DIFFERENT

DISTANCE

A

DIFFERENT

DISTANCE

a renga

MARILYN HACKER and
KARTHIKA NAÏR

MILKWEED EDITIONS

© 2021, Text by Marilyn Hacker and Karthika Naïr
All rights reserved. Except for brief quotations in critical articles or
reviews, no part of this book may be reproduced in any manner without
prior written permission from the publisher: Milkweed Editions, 1011
Washington Avenue South, Suite 300, Minneapolis, Minnesota 55415.
(800) 520-6455
milkweed.org

Published 2021 by Milkweed Editions
Printed in the United States of America
Cover design by Mary Austin Speaker
Cover art by Abi Daker
22 23 24 25 26 5 4 3 2 1
First Edition

Library of Congress Cataloging-in-Publication Data

Names: Hacker, Marilyn, 1942- author. | Karthika Nair, author.
Title: A different distance : a renga / Marilyn Hacker and Karthika
   Naïr.
Description: First edition. | Minneapolis, Minnesota : Milkweed
   Editions, 2021. | Summary: "Celebrated poets Marilyn Hacker
   and Karthika Naïr compose a collaborative poem marking a
   year of friendship through stillness and grief"-- Provided by
   publisher.
Identifiers: LCCN 2021029434 (print) | LCCN 2021029435 (ebook)
   | ISBN 9781571315519 (paperback) | ISBN 9781571317780
   (ebook)
Subjects: LCGFT: Renga.
Classification: LCC PS3558.A28 D54 2021 (print) | LCC PS3558.
   A28 (ebook) | DDC 811/.54--dc23
LC record available at https://lccn.loc.gov/2021029434
LC ebook record available at https://lccn.loc.gov/2021029435

Milkweed Editions is committed to ecological stewardship. We strive to align
our book production practices with this principle, and to reduce the impact
of our operations in the environment. We are a member of the Green Press
Initiative, a nonprofit coalition of publishers, manufacturers, and authors
working to protect the world's endangered forests and conserve natural
resources. *A Different Distance* was printed on acid-free 100% postconsumer-
waste paper by McNaughton & Gunn.

For Julie Fay, Mimi Khalvati, Karyn London, Deema Shehabi, and Kim Vaeth, who all kept the lights on at "a different distance." For Golan Haji, Norbert Hirschhorn, and Fady Joudah, physicians of the heart.

—MH

To the kith—near and far, white-coated and not—who kept me safe and (somewhat) sane through this last year.

—KN

A

DIFFERENT

DISTANCE

Crocus, primroses,
in locked-down Square Léopold
Achille. The plague spring.

Rana sent me a photo
of police on Hamra Street

enforcing curfew.
The boy I watched on the roof
of the refugee

squat was locked down already,
daily, among washing lines

—MH, 29 MARCH 2020

Daily lines burgeon
on Louis Blanc pavements, each sprout
five feet from the next:

human unblossoms outside
baker-butcher-grocers' doors.

One out for one in;
gloved, masked, sanitised before
and after each yield.

The pigeons strutting the same
sidewalks heed no distancing.

—KN, 30 MARCH 2020

"Distance between us . . ."
she wrote long ago, and then
made it permanent.

Charpentier, *Vêpres à la Vierge*
(while I'm doing the dishes)

on the comforting
old squat black CD player:
for a moment, there's

connection, if only with
that perplexed self, desiring.

—MH, 30 MARCH 2020

That desire for self
to be more, more than terra
firma for virus

settlements, begets fresh creeds.
Parisians grunt and wheeze praise

to Lord Jogging, while
roaming forlorn as our streets.
Romans hymn and drum

Volare from balconies.
Jack Bernhardt downs ten thousand,

yes, minutes of *Bones*—
libation of eyes and wits
to fair Agent Booth.

The right mantra for lúc lắc
spurs my quest across the net.

—KN, 31 MARCH 2020

4

Across the street, a
girl stands lengthily at the
window, smoking and

looking at empty sidewalks,
sun-soaked on April first.

I wished the tourists
would disappear. Now they're gone.
Watch what you wish for!

In purdah, in quarantine,
I dice one more aubergine.

—MH, 1 APRIL 2020

Aubergine, once more.
Braised, bartha-ed, basil-and-beef-
fried, in any form . . .

The thought invades aurous noons,
leaves sharp pugmarks on my dreams

these still-wintry nights.
Preschoolers play COVID-Age
tag in our courtyard:

not more than two at a time,
and "catch" with an out-flung glove.

—KN, 3 April 2020

6

We drove out to the
place they called Karantina
where crews of ships from

Europe once waited forty
days to be declared plague-free.

Desolate still, but
in a lonely high-rise, in
a vast gallery,

the ninety-year-old painter's
new gouaches, texts, tapestries.

Afterward, a huge
Armenian lunch in Bourj
Hammoud with my two

young friends, nobody knowing
quarantine was just starting.

—MH, 3 April 2020

Bedlam just started
here, N writes from New Delhi's
migrant worker camps.

How will they lockdown millions
who have neither doors nor roof?

Millions who must walk
many moons to reach a home
to self-isolate.

Prime Minister Modi bids
his nation to light candles.

President Macron,
meanwhile, warned us off facemasks
unless really ill.

Spring: the dearth, in my two lands,
of roses for all the graves.

—KN, 4 April 2020

Rose garden hidden
in the Square du Grand Veneur—
it's starting to bud,

but the gates are locked, only
kids from the logements sociaux

in the enclosure
peer through the grates, in strange,
bright April sunlight.

Here's a petition against
euthanizing the sick old.

—MH, 5 APRIL 2020

Sick and old: for Laure
and Serge, teens from Block D, I
now tick both boxes.

L—four-inch heels keen across
cobblestones—rushes to hold

open all our doors.
Their mom, though, no longer hails
me with nod and smile:

chemo-shorn, brow-less beings
in masks could spell one more germ.

—KN, 6 APRIL 2020

One more spell, one more
incantation—it's only
The Art of the Fugue

or Hildegard of Bingen
or Alice Coltrane: music

calms anxiety.
Abida Parveen sings
a Hafez ghazal,

cross-legged, eloquent hands . . .
I pick out a word or two.

—MH, 6 APRIL 2020

Two words, now, for me:
Hum dekhenge—We shall see.
Iqbal Bano soars

skyward on Faiz's refrain, and
something steelier than hope

lights the heart once more.
Heart that fluttered last evening,
stalled a few instants:

a frog in the throat these days
hearkens to beasts less winsome.

—KN, 9 April 2020

12

Ego, clawing beast:
with or without our selfhood,
beasts try to survive,

as does each isolate I,
newly dispensable, or

in the equation.
Lock up these, those, forever,
then open the doors.

I open late windows on
unnatural bright April.

—MH, 10 April 2020

Bright as this April:
Isa, flushed after cycling
from Pantin—risking

dour fines we none can afford—
brings me dorayaki, home-

made, with sweet red beans
crushed and flour ground by Nico,
who'd foraged for weeks.

Balm for my bile-deluged gut,
swaddling for sleep-deprived dreams.

Wajdi Mouawad writes
to his infant, unknowing
son: *Quoi dire de plus*

urgent que l'amour? Sometimes,
pancakes will do just as well.

—KN, 13 APRIL 2020

Pancakes, not huîtres,
phone calls, texts, instead of wine-
flavored exchanges

in the public privacy
of a café. Sautéed snow

peas, shallots, chicken,
wine anyway, but for one,
yesterday's bread, a

departing moon above roof-
dormers, now my horizon.

—MH, 14 April 2020

My horizon, each
week: the poppy-printed, teal
hair cap of Nurse Rose

(handstitched, the florets for cheer)
as she disinfects—"secures,"

in the martial cant
so dear to our president—
my portacath site.

She, of calm hands and raptor
gaze, snags any truant vein.

—KN, 15 April 2020

16

I play truant when
I go to the bakery,
or Russian roulette

for a baguette tradition,
une réglette de macarons.

I should be indoors.
Back inside I'm dizzy with
fear, but I eat one,

two, caramel macaroons.
"Look, we have come through." Who knows?

—MH, 15 April 2020

Who knows anything
today? Prefects, priests, pressmen,
physicians . . . no one.

Yet, wait, everyone we know,
or don't, dons shades of prophet.

Sun-drenched flowed the Quais
de Valmy and de Jemmapes
these last afternoons

while I brooded indoors with
Coke as cure and company.

—KN, 18 April 2020

Wolves accompany
me, a dream I'd like to have,
lope across a steppe,

howl an ode to the half-moon,
break bread with al-Farazdaq,

hunt mice if we must.
Overarching, the night sky
blankets the city

we're immured in, or opens
it up to ghazals of rain.

—MH, 19 April 2020

A rain of ghazals,
petrichor from verse by long-
lost poets, crumble

many sabre-toothed daymares,
if just for a rainbow while.

Ghalib, Faiz, Firaq,
Sahir (always Sahir), then
the doyen, Khusrau:

sufi, secular or plain
kafir; their ghazal, nazm, and

sher, the first to strike
my early, unlearned ears;
demand rebellion

yet earn adoration from
a resolute nastik heart.

—KN, 20 APRIL 2020

20

My atheist heart's
an impatient physician,
has no words to calm

vertigoes, palpitations
provoked by a sentence in

a news brief, or just
the sameness of spring days that
lengthen, out of reach.

No words then, music, numbers
and feeling, metal, thoughts, reeds:

oud, violin, or
saxophone, behind them
a mind, hands, a mouth

unseen as a friend's face now.
Today, the doctor's Mozart.

—MH, 21 APRIL 2020

My doctors Bourrat
and Blazy—Amazons with
spines of carbon steel,

shafts marked truth and solace,
fingers the envy of neat

goldsmiths—take the time
to write and ring, to enquire,
and devise relief,

with bad puns, in pandemics,
covering for painkillers.

—KN, 23 April 2020

Covering her face
with the mask she'll wear all night,
my daughter goes to

meet the patient first in the
queue: midnight in the ER.

Through nights in Aceh
after the tsunami, in
a hospital tent,

she saw herself back in school,
saw herself the physician.

I imagined her
then, now, at a different
distance, think of her

unmasking in the morning,
driving home to walk the dogs.

—MH, 23 April 2020

Home with the dogs—four—
and spouse of five-odd decades,
my dad (veteran

of three wars; child, too, of World
War II, famines, a blood-steeped

Partition) thunders
at the virus, the lockdown,
the distance from kin . . .

the years of command futile
before this covert agent.

—KN, 24 April 2020

Before, I covered
my head to enter a mosque.
I cover my face

now, to go down to the street.
Niqab's forbidden in France,

but masks like the ones
the kiné gave me will be
obligatory.

I sent a photo of my
solo atheist iftar

to Samira in
Algiers, to Maryam in
London. Next year will

we sit down together to
break bread for anyone's feast?

—MH, 26 APRIL 2020

Stale bread: feast for one
gleaning breath from rotting peel
and near-empty cans

of red beans from garbage bins
around the local Mono'p.

Streets abandoned by
traffic and pedestrians
find homes with vagrants.

Vagrants left unfed, unsafe,
even as the cops slap fines

on their unhoused hands,
and leaders applaud our state-
wide lockdown success.

Some deaths never figure, not
even as nameless figures.

—KN, 28 April 2020

Known, nameless faces,
figures, throw open windows
up and down the street

each night at eight to applaud
doctors, nurses, éboueurs,

and to show ourselves
to each other at the end
of a locked-in day.

I wave to the girl in the
fifth-floor dormer, she waves back.

—MH, 29 APRIL 2020

Her sixth-floor dormer,
a cigarette, the much-loved
view of our skyline:

Claire—critical-care intern—
sighs for one, after twenty

hours on breathless feet.
Evening applause is sweet, but
she'd choose PPE

over the President's praise—
and eggs on grocery shelves.

—KN, 1 May 2020

Shelves in the G20
are still filled with coffee, cheese,
brown eggs, garriguettes,

Greek yogurt, milk, wine—but I
hurry, forget tomatoes,

get out of harm's way
(masked, gloved) as fast as I can.
Food shopping once was

community, communion.
Poison in the chalice now.

—MH, 2 MAY 2020

In my chalice, now,
on good days: mouthful of fresh
cirrus and sapphire,

sometimes nimbus, with falling
sheets of vitreous heaven.

That daily ramble,
required to expel Taxol
and its unkind ilk,

impossible alone, yet
forbidden in company.

Once more, Doctor B
rides to the rescue, handing
armour to my knights:

Isa, Nico, Claire, Philippe
bear her letterhead as shield.

—KN, 4 May 2020

A facemask as shield,
or he hopes so, bearing wine
and some news, Hisham walks

along the Corniche, open
now, toward Raouché,

his mother's flat, where
he hasn't been in three months.
Scholarship, maybe,

fall term in London, maybe.
Freekeh bil dajaj tonight.

—MH, 4 May 2020

Tonight, an empire
of pain reigns over attempts
to write, think; to be.

Fall, even *summer*, graze past
ears as would submerged boulders.

RDEB—four
horseless, shapeless, ageless words
must play first fiddle;

second, third, and last, as well,
while all others earn exile.

—KN, 5 May 2020

Home becomes exile
in the punished city. Leaves
green beyond grillwork,

Nâzim Hikmet's postcard from
prison poems on the sill.

Locked-in lovers make
love until it bores them. Once,
through a hurricane

in Crete . . . but that was three days,
decades ago, two of us.

—MH, 7 MAY 2020

This, decades ago,
was how I gaped at the sea.
Reaching Rue Manin,

the years sublime, suddenly-
much-younger selves drink from this

downpour of gloaming,
we gasp at the carnival
corralled within Parc

des Buttes-Chaumont. Cedar, elm,
and linden; pine, plane, and beech,

arch towards the sky.
Hazelnut and cherry trees
flaunt wanton blossoms,

and the cascades underground
serenade us from afar.

—KN, 8 May 2020

From afar, but it
wasn't, thunder, rush of dark
clouds, then crash of rain,

just after I noticed, no
gates blocked the berges of the Île

Saint-Louis. No way
but, run under the torrents,
no café shelter.

Strip off once indoors, shower.
Flu, or worse, I'm on my own.

Later, on my own,
I slice shallots and mushrooms
into olive oil

and begin to imagine
I might not cough tomorrow.

—MH, 9 May 2020

35

Tomorrow might bring
the unknown—new foes, allies
of Taxol; blitzkrieg

within the chest; skull afire
(the mind sentinels one front

alone, these days)—but
also Philippe, bonne fée, by
the hospital doors,

strafed by showers or barraged,
joyfully, by vernal sun.

—KN, 12 MAY 2020

Lengthening vernal
afternoons to evenings,
sometimes we would walk

Bastille to Concorde, halfway
back, talking, stop for coffee

in a nondescript
café, touching each other's
arms for emphasis.

Where the métro took someone
home's a foreign country now.

—MH, 13 May 2020

Foreigners but both
home: this body and Paris,
the only ones I

have known dearly for thus long,
inconstant, heedless satyrs,

but mine, always mine.
Now, though, they turn hesitant,
unfamiliar to

their mirrors, shorn of birthmarks
and lush with other beings.

—KN, 14 May 2020,

Budding, lush, wilting,
lilacs, then roses, behind
iron grills: locked gardens,

each with some reminiscence.
There, we ate ham sandwiches

on a bench, talking
about Homs, and Aleppo.
There, a France Inter

reporter interviewed me
two months after I finished

chemo. I stared at
green leaves, blue sky, found something
more appropriate

to say than "I'm still alive."
And am, outside the gates, now.

—MH, 15 May 2020

Outside now, the sun
beckons—Piper whose descants
play louder than full

orchestras. Parisians hear
and obey, disregarding

dictates by doctors,
ministers, coppers, and throng
canal quays and squares.

Masks hang from chins, kiss pockets.
Distance is a banished land.

—KN, 17 MAY 2020

Banished from London
streets as over seventy,
Arij remembers

her mother's joy walking through
Zamalek, head bare, at last,

and going back nine
years ago to interview
Tahrir Square students.

She wraps an ironic scarf
to mask her face, and goes out.

—MH, 17 MAY 2020

"A face, a hand, or
chest: how long since I felt one
other than my own?"

Caregiver C, whose hugs could
lull most breeds of pain, sounds lost.

Back home for a few
prized hours, she cannot snuggle
her two young children,

just as distressed. Lou, the cat,
alone rubs against her feet.

—KN, 19 MAY 2020

I sip it alone,
Italian coffee with a
little cardamom.

Last time I drank coffee with
someone: my best student, at

Kaza Maza in
Hamra, before she left for
the mountains, with friends,

to play out the quarantine.
After she'd gone, I lingered.

—MH, 21 May 2020

Lingering after
the sun dives down nacreous
rooftops, I trace them—

chimney pots, dormers, the slate
tiles, the lead guttering—all

with distant, blackened
fingers that recall other
lines and curves. Breathing,

speaking ones, that reach out, and
not merely to note a pulse.

—KN, 22 May 2020

44

A day's pulse measured
sometimes in outgoing calls.
A voice but no face

accompanying. If I
meet a friend in the street, we're

both masked. Yesterday
Nahed bused to the Bastille—
we'd walk on the port.

Locked. On the Opéra stairs,
eyes, hands, enlivened masked words.

—MH, 24 MAY 2020

The words, unmasked, bear
serrated edges: "Relapse,"
says Doctor MM,

referring to her cancer.
It is I who flinch from them,

wishing I had not
just named the demons she'll have
to dispel once more;

named them and recounted all
their lurid powers at length.

—KN, 25 May 2020

The length of my life
now defines me like my skin
color, sex, or faith.

It's meant little since, aged five,
judged too young to read and write,

I said I could, did.
Again infantilized, should
I be locked up so

the young can go about their
business, getting and spending?

—MH, 27 MAY 2020

This business called
life got spent (say it: drained) on
just a glass of milk

at Muzaffarpur railway
station. Maqsood Alam—house

painter in Delhi,
banished back to his Bihar
by statewide lockdown,

by national uncaring—
"ran pillar to post" to save

his ailing Ishaq,
aged four. The boy's breath ran out
sooner than columns

to fill in the government-
drafted forms for sustenance.

Same day, same station:
a babe tries to wake his dead
mother. Police state

both died on trains. And that kin
still get ex gratia aid.

—KN, 30 MAY 2020

Still point of morning,
discarded masks on the street,
riots' detritus.

Not a morning of roses.
Patients on ventilators

echo "I can't breathe,"
or might if they could speak.
What's your death sentence—

counterfeit bill, métro ride ?
The knee comes down on your throat.

—MH, 31 May 2020

Throats, knees, lungs, kidneys—
dispensable, when cased in
black, brown . . . Dalit skin?

Ask Bondy-based Gabriel,
fourteen, who might lose an eye:

lawless justice from
Castaner's cops. Names, too, are
a kind of hide for

Larbi, their shades litmussed in
grillings at border control.

—KN, 3 JUNE 2020

Borders were porous
with the right passports
or a titre de séjour.

Danes can go to Norway now,
but Swedes can't. When Nahed got

her French passport, we
drank champagne. She can't see her
sister in Stockholm.

She's job-hunting in Toulouse,
going masked to interviews.

—MH, 5 JUNE 2020

Unmasked interview
on Crowdcast—isle of brief joy,
its sole borders those

carved by broadband access, land
with no COVID contagion—

where Meena and I
speak at the US launch of
her book *When I Hit*

You; speak of verse, fiction, caste
killings, murderous husbands,

and more; speak, across
·Boston, London and Paris,
with gracious Shuchi,

host from Brookline Booksmith, to
readers, unseen, round the world.

—KN, 8 JUNE 2020

From around the world,
Lebanese expats are flown
back to al-watan—

Moscow, Rio, Montreal,
Paris—bringing the virus

to their homecomings
in Beirut or the Beka'a.
Numbers leap. Katia

wrote to me a month ago:
Our epidemic's over.

I know she follows
the news . . . Cafés reopened,
clothing shops, crèches.

As for the money changers,
were their counters ever closed?

—MH, 10 June 2020

Close encounters, let's
call them, of the fifth or sixth
kind: in Bareilly,

returnee migrants get soused
with liquid bleach—yes, the kind

bottled with danger
to eyes and skin—as a cure,
by the State, no less,

while Delhi shuts hospital
doors on its nonresidents.

—KN, 12 June 2020

Resident of a
city, body, state of mind
I shrug off under

shadows and sun on the Quai
Saint-Bernard. A yoga class

salutes the river;
a portly couple tangos
to their own cassette.

I walk without a mask, as
far as the Jardin des Plantes.

—MH, 13 JUNE 2020

Assemblage, as far
as the eye can feed: litchi,
melon, mint, mango,

moka, peach . . . corps de sorbet
(and ice) glimmer and curtsy,

preen, swirl in their trays
to carouse with me, Isa
and Nico—plotters

of my first sortie outside
home and hospital. Lambent

this dusk, like our blithe
reunion at Berthillon,
Île Saint-Louis, still

Mecca for bon vivants, each
palate worshipful in queue.

—KN, 15 June 2020

56

In a queue for bread
outside the bakery on
the boulevard: it's

almost normal. An almost-
normal Sunday market with

hand sanitizer
dispensers at entrance points.
Almost no distrust

of the masked person next in
line for cherries, shrimp, courgettes,

hummus, samosas.
Which merchants have disappeared?
Which shoppers I knew

vaguely by sight won't I see
again? It's chilly for June.

—MH, 21 JUNE 2020

June, now, is the month
of solstitial nights, roses,
and two presidents

convinced the grandeur of their
nations—flanking, from north and

south, the Atlantic—
resides in statues of dead,
all-too-fallible

men, to be safeguarded far
more than the breath of today's

denizens; convinced
naming evils of the past
would be a crime (mine

christened it separatism).
How frail must they find our lands?

—KN, 27 JUNE 2020

Old, frail, nonetheless
I walked home from Montparnasse,
invulnerable

for the moment, pink K-way
against the drizzle. Almost-

midnight streets full of
mostly local, mostly young
drinkers and flâneurs

as if nothing had happened.
I kept my mask on, except

on the Pont Sully
where there was no one, only
reverberations

of music on the quais, next
Decamerons, next clusters?

—MH, 29 JUNE 2020

Clusters of colour—
reign of aestival blossoms—
caper on Philippe's third-

floor balcony. They join us
and a madcap even breeze

to celebrate this,
my first visit in many
months; first touch of drink

(organic) outside home and
hospital since early March.

—KN, 4 July 2020

"Since we want to march
from the hospital to the
BDL and set

up our tent, we should wear scrubs
and masks," Rachid said. Interns,

medical students
were planning one more sit-in.
"We'll be wearing masks

anyway," said Nour. "They found
forty new cases last night."

—MH, 6 July 2020

Another new case,
in our land: Martine Landry,
all of seventy-

six, Amnesty activist,
acquitted after three years

of legal nightmares
for her solidarity
to teen refugees

who'd have been wrongly expelled.
Oh, we take pride in being

playwrights of the great
Declaration of Human
Rights—but, it's a show

we'd rather tour or license
abroad than produce at home.

—KN, 10 JULY 2020

At home, my brain or
my blood churn out symptoms: stress,
swellings, dizziness,

unhinged by solitude and
anxiety. Telephone

calls replace dinners,
long walks down known, unknown streets.
We're free, but who's "we"?

It was a challenge in March.
Is it perpetuity?

—MH, 11 JULY 2020

"Is it already
the end?" That was from Nurse D,
distractedly, while

finetuning the drip flow to
my chest. *Already?* Six months,

or twenty-four weeks
and three days; I can spare you
the hours, but let's throw

in a pandemic for change.
Our laughter rings verdigris.

—KN, 18 JULY 2020

The grey-green eyes of
the floundered revolutions,
hers and his and hers,

wolves' eyes in a dream fading
to a blurred image of hills,

apricot orchards,
Beka'a Valley vineyards I
never visited—

Bukra fil-meshmesh, these years'
harvests of gone tomorrows.

—MH, 19 July 2020

Tomorrow has gone,
I learn, for Hasdeo Arand—
forest in central

India, haven for Gond
tribes, eighty-odd species of

trees, scrubs (thirty-eight),
herbs (nineteen), birds (one one one)
sloth bears, elephants,

leopards: larynx of a land.
Coal mines emerge. Through lockdown.

Standing committees
lie down, governments traffic
reserve forests, and

Adani makes hay while a
virus shines—blinding nations.

—KN, 20 JULY 2020

Four o'clock sunshine
on the Seine: the bookshop's a
beehive. Karthika

is here and I'm here, first time
we've met since January.

In a room above
the river, we record for
the Bengaluru

festival she can't attend.
Then we sit at Panis, with

hot chocolate, black
coffee. She takes off the mauve
silk scarf round her head

and lets the sun soothe the scars,
tease the hair-stubble to grow.

—MH, 26 JULY 2020

Stubbly the teasing,
the banter, the laughter—sweet
nothings we had grown

unused to, locked down all these
months. This reading-recording

first, with Marilyn
and Adam, and an unseen
pianist, upstairs

at Shakespeare and Company.
My favourite Wednesday

this year. Then, a slew
of retrouvailles—its English
sibling feeble—all

week, spotlit by the same sun
and, often, hot chocolate.

—KN, 31 JULY 2020

Foot, hot in its brace
for a stupid broken bone,
propped on a cushion,

I'm back and forth on WhatsApp
for six hours; two explosions

on the port, half of
Beirut blown up: Gemmayzé,
Bourj Hammoud . . . "We're safe,

in shock, the windows shattered . . ."
War-zone cell-phone videos.

The bride in white lace
hijab, blown down in her gown,
is a doctor who

was in an ER six hours
later, triaging stretchers.

—MH, 6 August 2020

The triage stretches
through the night on Kozhikode
Airport's tarmac, then

in ERs of hospitals
across two neighbouring towns.

Volunteers—battling
manic rains and a raging
virus—seek voices

beneath the debris of one-
ninety lives fleeing COVID-

19 from Dubai.
Eighteen dead, and one-twenty
injured. "Amma, were

there people you . . . ?" She replies:
"They were all someone's blood, child."

—KN, 9 August 2020

Someone's child, someone's
uncle, sister, son: were they
blasted, infected?

The disasters converge. While
Katia sends me a WhatsApp

photo, bottle of
white wine I left in the fridge
on Makdisi Street.

"I've packed your books and clothes. We'll
drink the wine when you come back."

—MH, 17 August 2020

"When you come next, we'll
drink a beaker of sunset
by Vellayani

Lake!" Then his voice clouds, "That won't
be likely this year, will it?"

Buoyant since birth, my
dad held on to hope all these
months: a surefire cure,

tests, vaccines . . . His belief, now,
flags after the morning news.

—KN, 23 August 2020

No more rainbow flags—
Les Mots à la Bouche bookshop
has been replaced by

another Doc Martens store,
and the Moroccan grocer

by Princesse Tam.Tam
underwear, one of three clones
in ten blocks. I don't

want to walk down the rue Sainte-
Croix de la Bretonnerie,

where sometimes I'd go
near midnight and browse, come home
with that new novel

by Nina Bouraoui and
grapefruit juice for the morning.

—MH, 23 AUGUST 2020

Grief stains the morning
like grape, overripe, the tongue:
purple, glutinous.

Grief stains their voices: Achan
and Amma live, relive, loss

each time I call. Three
deaths in two days: old, dear friends,
forty- and sixty-

year-old kinships; their markers
of being. Grief edged by new,

enforced distance, by
the lack of touch, of last rites.
Grief clogs, till Swaroop

YouTube-streams a funeral.
Life seeps back into their chords.

—KN, 31 August 2020

Who'll get their life back?
Although no one ever does.
Iva says the last

trip she took was seven months
ago, to a friend's wedding,

classmate from med school,
and no one's come to their house
since February,

though the big garden's in bloom.
You're the risk factor, I tease—

nights in the ER.
It's two years since I've seen her,
Beirut, night shifts, now

pandemic intimacies:
WhatsApp, FaceTime, telephone.

—MH, 4 September 2020

The old telephone
holds Larbi's voice, which holds me,
gently, as he says:

"Ron is no more. The end was
sudden." We'd thought, like him, *cure*

was a real word;
so is *relapse*, we learn. Ron,
wind beneath many

wings; our own counter-cliché—
the finance pro who loved dance.

"His eyes shimmied when
he spoke of performances
watched with you": gauche, my

words to Marcel, Ron's husband,
who brings me comfort instead.

—KN, 8 September 2020

76

Instead of teaching
online in the ruins of
Beirut, Rana flew

to Norway with her two kids,
back to her fourth language, their

school days, her research.
Abou Rana and his group
of leftist thou'ar

are on the street every night,
masked in the late summer heat,

clearing rubble in
Gemmayzé, whose tragedies
a year ago were

lovers leaving, or leases
with exorbitant new rent.

—MH, 11 September 2020

Exorbitant, new
fears raise Raavan-heads every
where; vie for first place

in the mouths of ministers
and media. We make room

for "séparatisme,"
and then "ensauvagement." My
parents taste "urban

naxal": should I tell them that
is bhakt-speak for folks like me?

—KN, 17 September 2020

Devotee of do-
nothing, the minister does.
In one another's

arms, faces, masks on chins, wrists,
the young crowd late-summer streets,

drinking Cokes or beer,
eating sandwiches. I wish
this were fine. I'd like

to mind my own business, read
film reviews, not virus charts.

—MH, 18 September 2020

I read film reviews,
famished for the cinema—
land unvisited

since March. And theatre, word
that makes me weep: patria,

no less, touchable
only during virtual
meetings, rehearsals

recorded and "WeTransferred"
(new terms that yield bread, though not

quite butter). Shambling
home from hospital, I watch
hounds, pugs, mutts, and pups

raise happy Cain by the quai:
enfin, a show safe for all!

—KN, 22 SEPTEMBER 2020

For all the good it
does, the mayors say "Stay safe,"
with no restrictions.

It's your fault if you're fat, old,
diabetic, asthmatic,

or having chemo.
Stay indoors. We'll keep the bars,
gyms, playgrounds open.

It's fall, it's started raining,
and the river says, "Elsewhere . . ."

—MH, 28 September 2020

Rivers of sunlight
flood Joëlle's studio, much
like faces, voices,

fill her screen—from Bangalore,
Delhi, Dhaka, Calcutta.

All gathered to fête
eighty years of Alliance
Française du Bengale.

And J and I, with demon-
tiger and forest-goddess,

join the party from
Ivry. Through verb and line, curve,
morpheme in three tongues.

The Sundarbans fill our mask-
less minds, and laughter, our ears.

—KN, 28 September 2020

Our minds, our ears, eyes
are dulled with grim statistics.
Not much else, except

the train wreck of the world as
we thought it might be: well-oiled

dictators, would-be
tyrants, armed thugs. Wildfires
blaze through rainforests.

We pretend it's la rentrée
here. Masked kids flutter like bats

in the street when school
lets out. Badauds throng café
terrasses for what may

be last times, before wind, rain,
or closure and confinement.

—MH, 1 October 2020

Confinement closes
in, rusty-tongued this time, but
still raptor: reminds

Dr. B, warning me of squalls
ahead. Her first respite in

nine months, "capsized," she
sighs, "by the rising caseloads."
Yet she can find cheer

in my reborn lashes and
brows, and laugh at poor sallies—

this week, mine feature
filet de breast, grilled extra rare
but served, alas, sans

sauce teriyaki (slathered
with bicain lotion instead).

—KN, 7 OCTOBER 2020

Lotion on my cheeks,
forehead, and neck—anything
soothing and calming.

Now that I can walk again,
take a walk after dinner.

Darken all the screens.
Drink red wine instead of white,
or no wine at all.

Tisane à la verveine be-
fore bed, harpsichord music,

maybe a hot bath,
though I had one at seven,
changed the bed linens.

Awake at three, five, at six
I get up, say it's morning.

—MH, 9 October 2020

Morning can get no
more rutilant than this. I
have seen it after

long. After seven months, three
weeks, a night. I counted each,

on the trail that led
here, to A. Boutrous's *One
More Thing*, at Théâtre

des Abbesses, to dancers, to
selves arcing, tumbling, torquing,

crouching . . . to twined limbs
and huddled heads and ragged
breath that invites mine

to sing, to thrill, to be once
more, once more be this instant.

—KN, 13 October 2020

An instant implodes
the insouciant afternoon.
It could be the bike

that glanced me crossing the street.
It could be long, honed knives.

My writing hand is
in plaster. The closing of
a mosque distracts from

the city under curfew.
Commuters rush home from their

obligatory
work to fixate on more screens,
complexions of fear.

I write on a screen, too, look
with longing at my notebook.

—MH, 20 October 2020

Notebooks and longing:
I think of notebooks, little
smudged, lined notebooks that

waited for aeons to gleam
with this chronicle, a date

and a name: 7
November 2020;
Kamala Harris.

Vice President-Elect. Light
streams into this year, in skeins.

—KN, 9 NOVEMBER 2020

Trout streams or jet streams,
duffel bag, binoculars:
life of "the wild old,"

as Marie imagined and
lived it in her seventies,

eighties. Stroke-silenced
her last decade, she didn't
live to see "old" mean

indefinite confinements,
wild like a wolf in a cage.

—MH, 11 November 2020

Uncaged, like wolf cubs
in the wilderness, bounded
our smiles. Last Thursday:

we met after four whole months,
only the third time this year.

Virtual, though, this
reunion, with our faces
mosaicked across screens

in UK by Zoom at the
Achates Philanthropy

Prize ceremony.
We read poems to honour
heroes who brought art

to homes through the pandemic.
#artfeltthanks, no mere slogan.

—KN, 18 November 2020

90

Slogans, jokes, went round
the first time, recipes for
iftars solitaires,

photos of cassoulet or
couscous, window-framed landscapes

of unconfined trees,
berges de la Seine, the Corniche,
Riverside Park dogs.

No one's clapping in windows
this time. Winter is coming.

—MH, 22 November 2020

This time, winter comes
to Paris on stockinged feet,
no fuss, no fireworks,

until she's layering breath
with frost and the pipes with gnarls.

In Vellayani,
my parents greet their wedding
anniversary

by bracing their windows and
ears for Cyclone Burevi.

—KN, 3 December 2020

Ears attuned to sounds
at three in the morning that
are irrelevant:

techno party down the block,
wine shop delivery truck,

the pulse in my ears.
And sleep is over again:
dream conversations

on the Corniche, Raouché's
wave-lapped rocks, kitchen table

that might be here or
some unvisited city.
Conversations stop

with the dreams; night continues
with its noises, my silence.

—MH, 5 December 2020

The noise, the noise shreds
all thought to silence. Inside
the dazzling white drum

("a cylindrical super-
conducting MR scanner,"

the radiographer
corrects softly), I am mere
atoms of water,

each captained by protons of
hydrogen, hurtling earthward.

Mere mass, off-kilter,
of drops rushing, lining, re-
aligning between

magnets and radio waves,
between rhythm and discord.

—KN, 12 December 2020

Discordant darkness
of curfew-emptied streets.
Saint Lucy's Day past,

daylight will linger longer,
but when will sidewalks refill

with people heading
to movies, theatre, dinner,
ou que pour flâner?

On a screen, I watched white-robed
girls crowned with candles, singing

"Santa Lucia"
in another country, in
another language,

another year, when voices
wove, anodyne, in the air.

—MH, 16 December 2020

95

They weave the air gold
today, the voices that brought
breath and heart this year.

Namesake-publisher at four
a.m.; then Jai and P, all

from Delhi. L ships
snowflakes from Boston; Honji
and Seb, red roses,

berries, and Lindt from Berlin.
Philippe, with choux à la crème,

lights up my landing.
Sankar, two decades on, smiles
his wishes by ten.

d, you'd said: "I know you know
you're loved." More than ever, d.

—KN, 18 DECEMBER 2020

What I loved more than
wine, pomegranate juice, or
cardamom coffee

was conversations. Her face
or his face, preferred language—

(mine was, often, a
shorba of three that seemed to
have its own grammar)

—and history, none the same.
I called Mimi today (she's

locked down in London)
and saw her silver mane, im-
perious nose, grin.

Thought of coffees and curries.
Voices, pages, feed us now.

—MH, 20 December 2020

Your voice on the page—
well, screens of laptop and cell
phone, if precise, not

poetic, we should be—feeds
me, d, with mirth, thought, joy, doubt,

absurdity, much
needed, through the galloping
months of this fearsome

time. Not everyone knows why
I have eluded faces—

Skype, Zoom, FaceTime, Whats-
App, whatever—whenever
possible. Last week,

I lost my voice. Tears unspooled,
instead, across video.

—KN, 23 DECEMBER 2020

Lights out across the
street, five stories of windows:
the young black-bearded

man at his computer screen,
the small, long-dark-haired woman

I remember as
a twenty-years-ago bride,
all eclipsed. And you

aren't far away, but the
Gare du Nord might be Beijing,

though if I launch a
bottle of syllables, one
will return on the

tide of the internet, in
one more possible morning.

—MH, 26 December 2020

One more loss to mourn:
Ousmane Sy, stage name Babson.
Soft-hearted giant,

says the press. King of the style
christened *House*, master mover,

choreographer,
champion of girl power.
Your *Queen Blood*, paean

to women, with eight danseuses-
dynamos, scythed space and time—

and a much-esteemed,
international jury's
presumptions. Come back:

you'd just begun, your brick-red
beats must sear sightlines for long.

—KN, 31 December 2020

Wouldn't the lines be long
at any clinic if they
vaccinated there,

and wouldn't it be worth the wait!
Instead, attente prolongée

alone, in winter,
nervous, in a cluttered flat,
waiting for the light

of day, of the next season,
of another person's face.

—MH, 4 January 2021

"Wear another face
this year," I tell two thousand
and twenty-one, "one

we'll fear less, if not quite love
at first sight." It lengthens, this

wait to be shielded,
like shadows at dusk. Or is
this the cotangent

the sun casts at dawn? The streets
of Paris, cobblestone and

bitumen and spit,
have no answers to give me,
as I tread from 10th

to 11th, 4th to 5th,
but they console: *We've seen worse.*

—KN, 8 January 2021

No worse, there is none.
Of course there is, but Hopkins
voices my mood at

three in the morning, awake
with head throbbing, sharp pain in

the small of my back.
Symptoms of distress, wanting
out, of confinement,

of laptop-screen dialogues.
Nahed's bright sublet, over-

looking cobblestones.
Mutabbal, bamya, Fairuz:
familiar, now so

strange I felt sick. Nahed walked
me, arm in arm, to a cab.

—MH, 11 January 2021

Let us arm ourselves
with memory, lest all trace
be swept under the new

bordel-de-merde level
of current chaos

with variant strains,
stagnant vaccination drives
and other tumult.

Before sunrise, January
9, outskirts of Calais: it's

minus three degrees
(Celsius) and masked police
are tearing up tents

of refugees, chasing them
to a hopeless, frozen dawn.

—KN, 13 JANUARY 2020

Hopeless to wait for
vaccine registration or
search for hours online.

A few fortunate ones signed
up: places filled in twelve hours.

So live your life in
suspension. Claire went for a
pedicure in a

Haussmannian flat, bought a
scone on the rue du Cherche-Midi

where we'd had lunch in
possible September. She's
ninety-five, seen worse,

unshelves Montaigne to reread
after she watches the news.

—MH, 26 JANUARY 2020

The news watched me back,
pleased, more pleased than Mister Punch
had ever been: *I'd*

dance with you if I could. Mark
the date, Rachid Ouramdane's

been named future head
of Théâtre national
de Chaillot, mecca

of dance in France. The heart sings.
Son of French-Algerian

parents, Rachid's coat-
of-arms at Chaillot for the
lustrum is one word,

hospitality, which he's
probed all these years. The heart sings.

—KN, 13 FEBRUARY 2021

My heart sinks as night
falls, minutes later daily.
Soon, March, spring again,

but *curfew, confinement* still
menace. "All this for a few

old farts who'd die soon
anyway . . ." comments in *Le
Monde*. I remember

the AIDS epidemic, shunned
gay sons. I'd rather be shunned

for flamboyant life
than "for my own good," I think
eating a salad

alone at nine o'clock for
the three hundredth COVID time.

—MH, 15 February 2021

The COVID Age: that
may be the Anthropocene's
gift to the planet.

My thoughts are dark, sometimes dour,
these vaccineless days and nights,

especially nights,
already overrun by
triffids, viciously

potent, tsars of vast terrains
of my body—mucous, skin,

· breath—now venturing
to occupy the lands I've
tried hard to defend

all these years. That space where word
meets page, that grand blank expanse.

—KN, 2 MARCH 2021

Expanse, constriction . . .
Marwan Barghouti has been
in jail for how long?

The Gazaoui student, at
Harvard on a fellowship,

goes out, gets coffee,
walks to the library, thinks—
but I don't know what

he thinks, only that he's there.
And I'm here, a constriction

round my temples, not
an occupying army,
only my weakness;

my body's vain protest at
its prolonged isolation.

—MH, 7 March 2021

It's been a prolonged
cosmic spoof, the quest to get
vaccinated: I'm

new kin to Don Quixote,
one whose windmills keep shifting.

Hospitals, barely
equipped to protect their own,
can't inject chronic

patients, despite trifectas
of RDEB, cancer,

and chemo, if we're
ambulatory. Vaccine
centres asked I turn

seventy-five. Today, I
savour post-vaccine fatigue.

—KN, 16 March 2021

"Fatigue, regrets . . ." a
quote from Adrienne Rich in
a notebook margin.

Once, twice a week, evening
conviviality, banned now.

One friend in the Lot,
one in the Vaucluse, with a
spouse/friend, watch seasons

change, take up gardening, hike,
ride bikes, study Italian—

Voltaire's dream? COVID
shuts the city down again,
possibilities

contingent on—but who knows?
Not budding trees, locked cafés.

—MH, 19 March 2021

Budding hope gets locked
once more. Caseloads skyrocket;
caregivers, frontline

workers fight, feet on quagmire,
less equipped a year later,

not more, despite all
the tedious talk of war and
wartime effort. Talk

comes cheap to our government,
talk that's a perfect smokescreen

for failure, torpor,
electoral ambition.
Islamo-gauchisme

gains screentime: great game
plan for twenty twenty-two!

—KN, 29 MARCH 2021

Two hours before dawn,
I give up on sleep, turn on
the bedside lamp, pick

up the book I put down at
midnight, attempt escape to

Algiers, another
decade, history, someone's
struggle who's not me

getting old in a quagmire
city, "Unfortunately

it was paradise . . ."
Solitary confinement
now. Food shopping the

only vestige of human
exchange, though daylight lingers.

—MH, 29 March 2021

What lingers, through day,
month, and year, will be kindness—
kindness that kept me

sane and safe, yes, even with
the same unsought trifecta

snapping at my heels,
noisy and unfunny, save
during our chats, d.

Scaffolding to laugh (and weep)
at this, the théâtre de

l'absurde of our own
grandly defective bodies.
In this almanac

of blessings, laughter became
you, d, and somehow, spring tide.

—KN, 31 March 2021

ACKNOWLEDGMENTS

We thank the editors of the following publications in which certain poems from *A Different Distance* first appeared:

> *Shakespeare and Company*
> *Los Angeles Review of Books*
> *Open Magazine*
> *Rusted Radishes*
> *Manhattan Review*
> *New England Review*
> *Michigan Quarterly Review*

KN: Words prove annoyingly inadequate here, as I attempt to thank the people who made this book possible. Some, directly, by bolstering the writing. Some held me together during this time, fraying threads, torn seams, and all. Some did both. Then there are those whose names I might not have caught, or retained: my fissures of memory or attention notwithstanding, their help mattered, mattered much. Among them all, in no defined order:

> Marilyn Hacker: for the very idea of the renga— and the invitation, which transformed this year; for patience, encouragement, and poetry that has been an inspiration for years;

> Fady Joudah: for the early, intent read, the impassioned discussions, and the catalytic belief in what would become *A Different Distance*;

Daniel Slager, Bailey Hutchinson, Mary Austin Speaker, Joanna (Yanna) R. Demkiewicz, Claire Laine, Milan Wilson-Robinson, and their teammates at Milkweed Editions: for welcoming the renga with warmth and certainty, and producing this book with elegant expertise;

Sarah Yake of Frances Collin Literary Agency and Angali Singh of Ayesha Pande Literary: for, once again, being our bridges across the ocean, and, once again, for priceless counsel;

Adam Biles: for organising a joyful, memorable recording session of the renga at Shakespeare and Company in July 2020; for the equally joyful afternoons, with little Anouk, of flânerie and literary dissections around Parc des Buttes-Chaumont through the "third wave";

Dr. Anne Blazy: for unstinting support, unsparing honesty, understanding; for startlingly inventive ways to beat or—at least—take on RDEB-triffids and chemo-gremlins; for the cheer, the shared fondness for wicked puns, the choice of orange-tinted footwear and accessories to brighten chemo-days, to assuage pain;

Rose Boudan: for her presence, through miles and miles of appointments, tests, surgery, chemo, radiation . . . ; for reorganising her holidays to ensure that presence through those miles; for the tact and gentleness deployed— across several departments of a large hospital—to get procedures programmed at the earliest, all without scuppering a long-awaited book tour; for gentle skill in finding elusive veins; for transfusions of optimism;

Dr. Emmanuelle Bourrat: for being a captain extraordinaire in EB research and care; for her rigour and dedication in coordinating that care across several departments and hospitals; for her attentiveness to all the related EB-critters, big and small, nipping at heels; for trying to ensure, always, that the disease does not submerge identity; for her delight in patients' achievements outside hospital;

Christine Chevrier, Hafsoiti Hassan Djohar, Isabelle Lafay, Christine Laborde, Célia Liron, Dr. Arnaud Rigolet, and their colleagues at Hôpital Saint-Louis; Dr. De la Dure-Molla, Judith Juste, and Dr. Paul-Armand Chaudru de Raynal at Hôpital Rothschild; Dr. Florence Zembra: for continuing to keep me somewhat functional, even these last eighteen months; for prompt help and resourcefulness in dealing with the triffids, which pullulated during this time; for immense generosity of time;

Dr. Mallika Amellou, Isabelle Assier, Dr. Bethsabée Benadon, Dalia Cissako, Dr. Hélène Corté, Hawa Dial, Samira Mezouar, Nadja Sondarjee, Honorine Villard, Dr. Stéphane Villiers, and others at the Sénopôle of Hôpital Saint-Louis: for joining forces with the teams above; for kindness and great reactivity; for shaping cancer treatment around the spiny contours of RDEB, as far as possible;

Dr. Golan Haji and Mr. Bhaskar Gopakumar: for breadth and generosity of knowledge; for the ability and patience to break down their knowledge into digestible bytes for non-professionals; for quiet support all through my mulish reactions to test results;

Philippe Bruguière: for being there, week after week, by hospital doors, after surgery, chemo, radiation, pain management . . . ; for staying back in Paris during all three lockdowns just for that; for farsightedly sourcing N95 masks right before they became rarer and dearer than a unicorn's mane; for endless treats of artisanal chocolate to mark each milestone of treatment; for engrossing discussions on Connected History and Indo-Persian syncretism through the music and miniatures, and so much more;

Sabine Kasbarian: for ensuring hospital pick-ups and drop-offs pre- and post-surgery these twenty years, despite their tiresomely increased frequency since 2020; for homemade tiramisu and crêpes as incentives for treatment; for taking me along to COVID-regulation-friendly, limited-access performances and dances whenever possible;

Isabelle Pichon-Varin and Nicolas Renault, Claire Delcroix, Stéphanie Harvier, Philippe Crespin, Martine Depagniat, Marielle Morin, Johanna Blayac: for vital, practical help and countless hours of vibrant discussion; for walking with me, literally and figuratively, since February 2020, armed with medical certificates—through lockdowns and fines, curfews and enthusiastic cops; for ensuring laundry—and pharmacy-runs, home maintenance, and grocery supplies while I could not; for scouring town to find essential provisions during the first, panicky phase of the lockdown; for a steady stream of delicacies, from homemade dorayaki to brioche to matcha cubes encased in dark chocolate, in a bid to retrieve the kilos lost to chemo.

Françoise Gillard: for bringing *Le Tigre de Miel* to magical life on the digital platform of the Comédie-Française; for frequent reminders that there was still more to the year than a dysfunctional body; for supplies of excellent confectionery and thought;

Mélanie Aron, Éric Auzoux, Marion Bastien, Chantal Berthoud, Willy Cessa, Awatef Chengal, Ginette Dansereau, Caroline Delaporte, Lies Doms, Oonagh Duckworth, Emmanuelle de Varax, Fabienne Gaudin, Christine Gurreri, David Jays, Girija Kaimal, Mira Kamdar, Wanjiru Kamuyu, Christine Lalou, Charlene Lim, James O'Hara, Daisy Phillips, Marek Pomocki, Dawn Prentice, Sunithi Bhandari and Lakshman Rao, Nicolas Six, Isabella Spirig, Laurie Uprichard, Françoise Vanhems, Cécile Vasseur, Honji Wang and Sébastien Ramirez, Laetitia Zecchini: for being only a phone call, or parcel, or—whenever possible—a sanitised visit or rehearsal away, whatever the latitude; for sending food for laughter and thought and, inevitably, taste buds;

Christine Cornet, Bruno Plasse, Jill Schoolman, Emma Raddatz, Sophie Giraud, Joëlle Jolivet, Dominique Vitalyos: for exciting new literary projects and suggestions, all through this time; for vast reserves of cheerful energy;

David Shulman: for the solace and music of *The Inner Life of Dust*; for a glimpse of the magical realm of Panchabhuti kriti; for the quiet, sustained inspiration that he and his comrades at Ta'ayush and the shepherds and cave-dwellers in the South Hebron Hills embody, against all odds, in the face of increasing violence and systemic injustice;

Claire Verlet, Delphine Dupont, Alexia Pick of Théâtre de la Ville: for access to some of the year's most unforgettable moments of dance; for the heady rush of being a tiny, writerly, translator-ly cog in the brave, bespoke world of a digital Danse Élargie;

Farooq Chaudhry: for the carte blanche that led to *Where Dragons Dance* taking shape in my head, which is what matters the most;

Gert Van Overloop, Irina Levskovskaya, Jonas Schildermans, Christine Tinlot, and my other colleagues at Eastman: for keeping me embedded in Larbi-land all through the trifecta of Cs; for the biggest box of Pierre Marcolini chocolates to go astray twice before arriving in Louis Blanc three months after dispatch from Antwerp, adding

weight to our own variant of Murphy's Law—and
to general merriment; for good-heartedness;

Sidi Larbi Cherkaoui: for continuing the tradition of
six impossible things before breakfast; for the beauty
and chaos, the doubt and the conviction; for making
work that—nearly two decades of familiarity later—
provides oxygen, punches the gut, and brings a song
to my heart, sometimes (as with the timeless *Faun*) all
at once;

Eva Kleinitz, Svetlana Rouveure, Ron Deckers: for the
courage and grace and honesty they exemplified, even
on the worst of days; for having been a part of my life,
and shaped it; for still, in many ways, being there;

Swarup B.R.: for irreverence and uncondescending
wisdom; for volunteering to keep alarmingly sociable
parents out of trouble during a pandemic; for tracing,
and liaising with, architects and accountants and
tile-layers, for two sets of distant, fastidious kin;

Pramod Kumar K.G.: for being, encore et toujours; for
celebrating this book although none of it, for once, was
written at his dining table; for all the book hampers sent
for fabular research—and solace;

Anand Murty, Rahul Soni: for happy misanthropy
and terrible music videos, and the ability to hold long,
droll conversations through iMessages;

Sankar Mohan Radhakrishnan: for the reliable reg-
ularity of our conversations, which were a soothing
reminder of things the pandemic did not upend;

Jai Arjun Singh: for continued Mahabharata-
obsession, this time transmuted into a course on its
stage and celluloid adaptations; for the many hours
spent preparing for the course, especially those
marvelling together at Mayabazar, for reading and
insightfully responding to, myriad writing, from gal-
ley proofs to early, unfinished drafts;

Nilanjana Roy, Salil Tripathi, Prem Panicker,
Karthika V.K., Ajitha G.S., Anita Roy: for writing
and calling, systematically, caringly, from various
parts of the globe; for roping me into their literary
ventures, long-distance;

Amma and Achan: for reading Vaikom Muhammed
Basheer's *Mathilukal* to me over Skype, thus bridg-
ing both distance and time; for their unconscious
reminder that the pandemic should not determine
some equations;

Deepak Unnikrishnan: for prose that coruscates,
each time; for gallons of Apple Cloudy and anecdotal
goodies that alchemised a six-hour airport wait; for
the ghastly awesomeness that is Onam Bo-Che,
and other unusual—yet effective—analgesics, like
a post-post-post-modern photo portrait of Casper-
the-ghost-via-Munch to combat nausea; for the space

and time, the breath, to acknowledge exhaustion, despair, and galactic levels of unknowing;

Sanjoy Roy: for remaining my 3:00 a.m. person, the pandemic notwithstanding, not just on design and layout and form and structure, whether in poetry or dance or now prose, but when triffids strike; for the wicked blood-brain barrier breaches; for the dispatch of fictional chocolate/dragon delights, in the absence of shared meals in either of our cities.

MARILYN HACKER is the author of fourteen books of poems, including *Blazons* and *A Stranger's Mirror* (longlisted for the 2015 National Book Award); a collaborative book, *Diaspo/Renga*, written with Deema K. Shehabi; and an essay collection, *Unauthorized Voices*. Her eighteen translations of French and Francophone poets include Samira Negrouche's *The Olive Trees' Jazz*, Jean-Paul de Dadelsen's *That Light, All at Once*, and Claire Malroux's *Daybreak*. She is a former editor of the *Kenyon Review* and of the French literary journal *Siècle 21*. She received the 2009 PEN Award for Poetry in Translation for Marie Etienne's *King of a Hundred Horsemen*, the 2010 PEN/Voelcker Award for her own work, and the international Argana Prize for Poetry from the Beit as-Sh'ir/House of Poetry in Morocco in 2011. She lives in Paris.

KARTHIKA NAÏR is a poet, fabulist, and librettist whose books include *The Honey Hunter*, illustrated by Joëlle Jolivet. *Until the Lions: Echoes from the Mahabharata*, her reimagining of the foundational South Asian epic in multiple voices, won the 2015 Tata Literature Live Award for Book of the Year (Fiction), was shortlisted for the Atta Galatta Prize, and was highly commended in the 2016 Forward Prizes. Naïr has scripted and co-scripted performances for choreographers Akram Khan (*DESH*, *Chotto Desh*, and *Until the Lions*, adapted from her own book), Sidi Larbi Cherkaoui and Damien Jalet (*Babel 7.16*), and Carlos Pons Guerra (*Mariposa*). She is the co-founder of Cherkaoui's Antwerp-based dance company, Eastman, and executive producer of several of his and Damien Jalet's works. She lives in Paris.